Assemblies Mad

Other Classmates:

2nd Series
Successful Subject Co-ordination – Christine Farmery
Parent Partnership in the Early Years –
Damien Fitzgerald
Playing Outdoors in the Early Years – Ros Garrick
Homework – Victoria Kidwell
Getting Promoted – Tom Miller
ICT in the Early Years – Mark O'Hara
Creating Positive Classrooms – Mike Ollerton
Getting Organized – Angela Thody and
Derek Bowden
Physical Development in the Early Years –
Lynda Woodfield

1st Series
Lesson Planning – Graham Butt
Managing Your Classroom – Gererd Dixie
Teacher's Guide to Protecting Children – Janet Kay
Tips for Trips – Andy Leeder
Stress Busting – Michael Papworth
Every Minute Counts – Michael Papworth
Teaching Poetry – Fred Sedgwick
Running Your Tutor Group – Ian Startup
Involving Parents – Julian Stern
Marking and Assessment – Howard Tanner

Assemblies Made Easy

Victoria Kidwell

continuum
LONDON • NEW YORK

Continuum

The Tower Building	15 East 26th Street
11 York Road	New York
London SE1 7NX	NY 10010

British Library Cataloguing-in-Publication Data
A catalogue record for this book is available from the British Library.

ISBN 0–8264–7199–4

Typeset by BookEns Ltd, Royston, Herts.
Printed and bound in Great Britain by
Antony Rowe Ltd, Chippenham, Wiltshire

Contents

Contents

Contents

Introduction: Why this Book?

Is this you?

Panic!

Me? Do an assembly? Nothing could have prepared me for the sheer terror that swept through me when my headmaster made this outrageous and unprecedented suggestion. I was destined for a fortnight of insomnia and adrenalin-filled creativity. The headmaster could have patented his sentence as an antidote for Immodium.

Writer's breezeblock

My trusty blank page of A4 paper and I communed regularly. My companion retained its blank status. So did my mind. I just didn't know where to start.

Dare to be different

I didn't want it to be a humdrum affair. There's always the temptation to download assemblies from the Internet or to do one out of a book. If that's what you want to do, stop reading now! In my experience, however, such assemblies never really work as well as those that are 'homemade': they're formulaic and never strike a true chord with the spectators. Neither can they possibly reflect the talents or foibles of the pupils who are going to perform them. Once, I had a pupil in my class who could do an amazing impression of a garden strimmer, and I was determined to incorporate that into one of my creations. My assembly was going to be memorable and, above all, valuable. I definitely intended to include humour but I also wanted to keep my job. A very fine line would have to be drawn. I wasn't quite ready for my P45. Yet!

Stage fright

Others delight in performance. Not I! At the risk of gross understatement, I do not relish performing in public in any form. When I gave a speech at my sister's wedding, my general demeanour would have given me a scholarship to the Betty Ford Clinic.

The prospect of standing in front of a potentially hostile or, even worse, bored audience held no appeal at all. This was very illogical as I'd been standing in front of every single member of it in my classroom for three years and had suffered no ill effects whatsoever.

Irreligious and unreligious

I do not believe in any god(s). Yet I do believe in promoting the 'moral values' and sense of spirituality that are inherent in all *reputable* religions.

If that was all I had to do, I would have felt more comfortable. However, government guidelines state clearly that assemblies should involve an element of 'collective worship' and be of a broadly Christian nature. Argh!

My distinct lack of religious conviction made matters worse. I make Posh Spice look like a Home Counties Maharishi. I did not feel at ease at the prospect of spouting prayers to an entity in which I didn't believe and I didn't fancy coercing the pupils into doing so either. I had previously watched their faces during the words: 'Let us pray ...' and 'This morning, I'm going to read you a passage from the Bible ...'. Valium (or euthanasia) could only aspire to produce such an effect.

If all of the above describe your mental state now that you're faced with 'doing one', I hope to address most if not all of your anxieties. You are not alone!

Think positive!

When you have successfully performed an assembly, everyone will have benefit – including you. I would also argue that the most reluctant participants profit the most – including you.

1

Preparation

If you suffer from the afflictions listed in the Introduction, then preparation is vital. This is the hardest and most important bit. The little grey cells will have to be in overdrive, and the self-discipline wil have to be autocratic.

The best way to prepare yourself mentally is to give yourself plenty of time, if that's at all possible. Ideally, write a few emergency assemblies and file them under 'Secret Weapons'. Don't lose them, as I've done!

Tips

Here are a few to get you started:

◆ work out what you want to say.

◆ summarize it in either one word or a very short sentence.

◆ write down *anything* that's related to your idea that comes into your head.

◆ plan your route to your main point.

◆ it *doesn't* have to be a direct route – diversions and asides make your content more interesting.

- write your route down in full, avoiding overlong sentences and superfluous adverbs and adjectives.

- revise content and add humour wherever you can.

- make sure your language is comprehensible to *all* your audience.

- vary the pace.

- time your speech and edit ruthlessly, bearing all of the above in mind.

Try to relax while writing and let your ideas flow. Don't worry if you write complete gobbledegook to start with. It happens.

2

Sources for Ideas

Useful equipment: a glass of wine, and a propensity for random and/or eccentric thought patterns.

Ideas come from everywhere. A former colleague of mine, who was sickeningly calm about these things, gave a superb impromptu assembly about his leaking flat roof (it was along the lines of 'Don't put off until tomorrow what you can do today'). Here are a few rich seams of inspiration that I have found handy over the years.

Newspaper articles

These may be of local, national or international interest. The ones I have found particularly useful are those very short and amusing news items in the weekend newspapers. For example:

- The man who fell out of his attic window. He fell three floors, bounced off a shop's canopy and into the river. Fortunately, he was unscathed. All he had been doing was trying to swat a fly. (Look before you leap!)

- The story of the two pigs, 'The Tamworth Two', who escaped from an abattoir. (Where there's a will, there's a way!)

The editorial section and readers' letters of local newspapers are also quite revealing of current preoccupations, and you can easily adapt these to your own ends.

Issues arising out of everyday school life

School events and issues are a fantastic starting place for assemblies, anything from Sports Day to achievements by individual pupils or members of staff. Here are some examples:

- Following Sports Day, one colleague did an assembly on perseverance.

- We interviewed another member of staff after he had been trekking in the Himalayas for charity.

- Litter had been a problem in the school. We invented a superhero character called 'Binman'. To play him, we deliberately chose a 'cool' (and rather handsome) member of Year 10, who wasn't afraid to make a spectacle of himself. That way, we got *everyone's* attention.

Proverbs

These are a brilliant resource, especially if you want to give a memorable and strong message without going down the religious route. I have done countless assemblies using proverbs as a starting point. It is very easy to relate them to the pupils' own experiences. There are countless gems to choose from, but the following are particularly helpful: a rolling stone gathers no moss; never judge a book by its cover; you can lead a horse to water, but you cannot make it drink; empty vessels make the most sound; the end justifies the means; every man is the architect of his own fortune; strike while the iron is hot; the devil finds work for idle hands.

Some proverbs, however, would be a bit of a challenge and/or deliciously inappropriate. I can't resist sharing these with you: a live dog is better than a dead lion; life isn't all beer and skittles; when all fruit fails, welcome haws; it is merry in hall when beards wag all; every elm has its man.

The pupils themselves

Your young charges are very valuable assets when pondering assembly topics. I suppose it's a bit like market research. They will tell you what issues are concerning them, both inside and outside school. Past examples have been: bullying (by far the most frequently suggested. It may be a challenge finding a fresh angle on this topic, but I'm sure your spectators will appreciate your efforts); a school rule with which they disagree and/or flout regularly (uniform, homework and chewing gum spring to mind); a favourite charity they would like the school to support; environmental issues; animal rights; child poverty; human rights; capital punishment.

Chatrooms of children's documentary and current

affairs programmes are excellent for finding out about the topics on which they're pondering.

Pop songs

Chosen carefully, these are wonderful for finding a theme for your creation. If you need to 'pad out' your offering, then play the music at the beginning and the end as well as during the assembly. It sets the subject and allows the pupils to mull it over. After all, government guidelines demand that collective worship should be a time for 'prayer and reflection'. If it allows you to kill a few minutes too, then that's a bonus! In the past, I have used: 'You bring out the best in me', Bread; 'Lazy', X-Press 2 and David Byrne; 'Always look on the bright side of life', Eric Idle and the Monty Python team (*very* carefully edited – I once forgot there were rude bits!); 'Bridge over troubled water', Simon and Garfunkel; 'Days of our lives', Queen; 'Sadness Part I', Enigma (adds a bit of gravitas to the whole procedure!).

During my research, I came across a few songs that would have caused uproar and led to my professional demise: 'In da Club', 50 Cent; 'Like a Virgin', Madonna (not even at Christmas!); 'My Ding-a-ling', Chuck Berry; 'Sex on the Beach', T-Spoon.

Events in your own life

I have spared them the gory details of marital mayhem, speeding offences and my less salubrious extra-curricular activities. However, this really is an excellent path to do down. The pupils really appreciate any snippets of personal information that you'd care to share with them. These can be more serious moments or, preferably, ones that show you in an embarrassing or vulnerable light. They might even start to believe you're human. At the risk of total humiliation, I'll cite but a few:

♦ Stories about my children when they have made me feel 'publicly uncomfortable'.

♦ Admitting that I once missed a flight by setting the alarm clock incorrectly, because my counting backwards skills are not what they should be, as a highly qualified professional.

♦ The morning I waved at a bin bag, thinking it was a friend of mine.

♦ The time I drove through my local town with a full coffee cup on top of my car – quite a feat, I think you'll agree! I couldn't understand why the rain was brown. (I have recently topped this by setting off at high speed with a large sponge cake on the roof.)

♦ Regrets that I may have, such as taking people for granted until it was too late to do something about it.

♦ Opportunities that I have missed.

Dreams

It's great fun to explore the meanings of dreams. You can approach this from a variety of angles. A good way is to present dreams as your subconscious mind trying to tell or warn you about something. Have a browse through one of many books or websites on the subject and you won't be short of ideas.

Stories and fairy tales

All age groups love stories and fairy tales. Younger children will enjoy them just for the sheer joy of hearing the plot. Older pupils will appreciate the hidden meaning behind the stories, and there are some fascinating books on this subject. For example, one can see *Alice's Adventures in Wonderland* as a metaphor for a girl's journey through adolescence, from idle childhood to conscientious adulthood. First, Alice must learn the rules that are essential for a civilized, adult life. Next, she must learn to apply them thoughtfully. Following them blindly would create anarchy, where there are no rules at all, as is demonstrated when she goes to see the Queen of Hearts and the Mad Hatter.

Current affairs

These are good too, especially for 'emergency assemblies'. Letters pages in newspapers and magazines are particularly useful. You can turn almost any event into a school assembly topic: local and general elections or referendums; political issues/scandals; water rationing; celebrities' latest antics; sport; stories involving animals; current local/national campaigns; acts of terrorism.

Major world events

You have to choose these quite carefully as it can make for quite a depressing start to the morning, and I try not to do depressing – leave that to your more lugubrious colleagues! Personally, I think I'd make an exception if I were doing an assembly on September 11th. Here are some examples: scientific discoveries; globalization issues; peace initiatives; interesting developments in other countries; major global challenges, such as a woman sailing single-handedly round the world or one of the ubiquitous hot air balloon endeavours; the merits of economic sanctions.

The Christian calendar

Obviously you could observe the major Christian holy days and festivals: advent; Christmas; circumcision of Jesus; Epiphany; the conversion of St Paul; the Purification of Mary; the Annunciation of Mary; Lent; Invention of the Cross; Easter; Rogation; Ascension; Transfiguration; Whitsun; Trinity; Nativity of the Blessed Virgin Mary; Holy Cross Day.

Typically British days of the year

It can be quite interesting to highlight the history of certain days of the year. Often their origins are completely unknown to staff and pupils alike.

St Valentine's Day

Valentine's Day originated in fifth-century Rome as a tribute to a third-century bishop, St Valentine. Previously, the Romans had observed a pagan celebration in mid-February to the god Lupercus that marked young men's rite of passage. Some believe this involved a lottery in which the young men would draw the names of teenage girls from a box. These girls would be the sexual partners of the boys for the following year.

One version of the St Valentine story claims that Pope Gelasius, obviously a bit of a party pooper, disapproved of this pagan ritual. Instead of drawing out the name of a girl, each boy would end up with the name of a saint. Rather than having their wicked way with a girl for a year, the boys were instructed to emulate the ways of the saint they had been assigned – not nearly as much fun.

Poor old pagan god Lupercus was given the chop as god of love. St Valentine got the job. The Emperor had removed Valentine's head somewhat forcibly in 270 AD because he had secretly carried out marriages between soldiers and their sweethearts. The Emperor believed that married men made poor soldiers and banned marriage from his empire. (Quite reminiscent of the English Cricket Board and the Australian Tour.) In a rather unwise move, Valentine tried to convert Claudius to Christianity. As a reward for his efforts, he was stoned and beheaded.

Mothering Sunday

This seems to originate in the seventeenth century.

Celebrated on the fourth Sunday in Lent, it began as a day when servants and apprentices could go home for the day to visit their mothers. They brought a 'mothering cake' as a gift.

By the nineteenth century, the observance of Mothering Sunday had almost completely died out. Thanks to the greeting card industry, it is now alive and well, along with Father's Day and, no doubt at some point in the future, Hamster's Day and Garden Hose's Day.

Shrove Tuesday

In the Anglo-Saxon *Ecclesiastical Institutes*, it states: 'In the week immediately before Lent, everyone shall go to his confessor and confess his deeds and the confessor shall so shrive him.' Sounds like a barrel of laughs! Shrove Tuesday is the Tuesday before Ash Wednesday and, therefore, the beginning of Lent. A day of penitence and spiritual cleansing. A kind of inner Toilet Duck. No wonder pancakes are so popular.

Ash Wednesday

Sadly, nothing to do with nicotine or barbecues. Hardly selling itself, Ash Wednesday begins a time of sober reflection, self-examination and spiritual redirection. Oh dear.

In the Good Book, it says: 'Jesus retreated into the wilderness for forty days to prepare for his ministry. It was for Him a time of contemplation, reflection and preparation.' Sounds like an inset day!

By observing Lent, most Christians join Jesus on His retreat. In ancient times, people marked times of fasting, prayer, repentance and remorse by placing ashes on their foreheads. This custom originates in Judaism. (See 2 Samuel 13:19, Esther 4: 1–3, Job 42:6 and Jeremiah 6:26.)

Maundy Thursday

Maundy Thursday is the last Thursday before Easter and seems to involve lots of foot washing, alms giving and munificence, with a dash of bread and wine. Christians remember it as the day of the Last Supper and when Judas betrayed Jesus in the Garden of Gethsemane.

The word 'maundy' comes from the Latin word for 'commandment', and relates to the command Jesus gave that we should love one another, feet and all. The royal family muscled in on maundy at Knaresborough in 1210. King John handed out money, clothing and knives. Royal foot washing does not seem to have started until 1730. It did not last long and James I was the last one to go anywhere near poor people's feet, with or without a barge pole.

An elaborate and colourful ceremony, the Royal Maundy is steeped in tradition. Usually at a large cathedral, worthy, deserving pensioners receive Maundy Money. This involves one man and one woman for each year of the sovereign's age. I wonder if it's tax deductible. The senior citizens get red and white purses, made especially for the occasion. The red purses contain money and the white ones contain coins made to commemorate the occasion.

April Fools' Day

Or All Fools' Day to some. The earliest record of this tradition was in France in 1564. Prior to that year, the New Year was celebrated for the eight days preceding 1st April. In 1564, the Gregorian Calendar was introduced and New Year's Day was moved to 1st January. This news took years to filter through as it was delivered on foot. Some recipients of the news did not believe it and continued to celebrate the New Year on 1st April. They were ridiculed by the rest of the population and became the butt of practical jokes. This evolved into a tradition of prank playing on 1st April, spreading throughout Europe and even to the American colonies (I bet they weren't ironic pranks!).

May Day

May Day seems to be about the only pre-Christian festival that hasn't been tampered with by the Church – apart from the fact that they keep moving Easter around so that the Bank Holiday occurs during term time and cannot be fully appreciated.

Rather than joyriding and terrorizing corner shop assistants, the youth traditionally spent the eve of May Day in the woods. The following morning they would emerge, singing carols and prancing around in greenery they had collected. They would collect money from the villagers. Hush money? Sometimes they would make a maypole and this would form the centrepiece for village activities. The focus was on dancing and pageantry – an expression of community solidarity rather than some fertility ritual. Somehow the maypole loses its suggestive symbolism. Disappointing. I wonder what Morris dancers make of that!

There are various theories about the origin of May Day. Some people believe it all began with the druids, who were into tree worship. Others veer towards the idea that it goes back to the spring festivals of Egypt and India. Then, there's the Roman festival of Floralia, when the Romans gathered spring flowers to honour the goddess of springtime, Flora.

Saint Swithin's Day

A mediaeval precursor to the Meteorological Office:

St Swithin's Day, if thou dost rain,
For forty days it will remain.

A cheery soul, St Swithin asked to be buried where 'passer-by might tread on his grave and where the rain from the eaves might fall upon it'. Ninety-nine years later, his body was moved to Winchester cathedral, whereupon it rained for many days.

Christian Saints' Days

There are countless hosts of saints from whom to choose. Obscure, quirky ones with eccentricities and weird life stories are particularly entertaining. For younger children, the stories in themselves are entertaining and informative. For older age groups, you can draw morals from biographies of the saints. Saints are also associated with crafts and professions.

A good investment is *The Oxford Dictionary of*

Saints (Farmer), which gives you all the juicy details. Alternatively, just tap the relevant name into an Internet search engine, or look at the Saints' Days calendar on *www.cafod.org.uk*.

Festivals from other religions and countries

These make interesting starting points for assemblies. Please note that the dates of these festivals vary from year to year, so you will have to check the exact dates yourself. A useful website is: *www.support4learning.org.uk*

European National days

By this, I don't necessarily mean national saints' days – we pedagogues have tended to flog these to death. National days from other countries can be a sound basis for an original and informative assembly.

Gimmicky National days

A quick perusal of newspapers, television and the Internet will show you which other national days are coming up. They set out to make us all more worthy beings and, therefore, are ripe for the picking when it comes to assemblies. Here are some examples: National Poetry Day; National Breast Cancer Awareness Day; National Non-Smoking Day; Make a Difference Day; National Curry Day; National Day of

Hope; National Take Your Daughter into Work Day; International Women's Day.

You can acknowledge other significant days too, such as Mothering Sunday, Fathers Day, All Saints' Day and, obviously, Halloween..

National weeks

Many organizations arrange special weeks in order to deliver their message to as wide an audience as possible. These are particularly handy if you're saddled with a whole week of assemblies. Here are some examples: National Week of Student Action (arranged by Amnesty International); National Health and Safety Week; National Library Week; National Chemistry Week; National Dark Sky Week; National Science and Technology Week; National Family Week; National Pet Week.

Many of these have websites and publicity materials that would provide ample food for thought.

Raising money for charitable causes

Despite the adverse publicity, 'Yoof' feel very strongly about some causes and are more than willing to try to motivate their peers. You could base a whole assembly on the work of a charity and fundraising initiatives could arise as a result.

Famous people

In our celebrity-obsessed culture, there's always some trivia that you can adapt into a diverting few minutes. As I write, David Beckham's new hairstyle would beg the question: how important is appearance? How do other people's appearances affect us? A peremptory browse through a history book or an Internet website will reap rewards. How about these famous figures: Nelson Mandela; Martin Luther King; Rosa Parks; Steve Beco; John F. Kennedy; Rene Vietto; Haile Selassie; Evelyn Glennie; Ellen MacArthur; Paula Radcliffe; Emma Richards; J.K. Rowling; Kofi Annan; absolutely anyone.

Recent sporting events

You're spoiled for choice here – there's always something going on. Right now, I can choose between the FA Cup Final play-offs and the fact that, amid much controversy, a woman is playing in an open golf tournament. What about the merits of the new 'Silver Goal' rule? Every summer, the extortionate prices paid for players raises the question of the responsible use of money. Sporting issues can raise a multitude of moral discussion points.

The Bible

I'm not a Christian, but I'm the first to admit what a fantastic storybook the Bible is. I would aim to use some of the lesser-known parables, such as that of 'New wine for old skins'. Ideally, I'd ask a few pupils to act the story out rather than read it, in order to avoid any comatose cases amongst the audience. The Book of Proverbs is superb.

You can also use the Ten Commandments and/or their equivalent in other religions. I tend to avoid the adultery one, especially if it's a Key Stage 1 audience.

Ancient mythology

The antics of the Greek and Roman gods can provide a good source of material, as the stories often carry an underlying message. Works of literature are also useful. I studied Ovid's *Metamorphoses* at school, which are full of morally enriching tales.

The seven deadly sins

Six of these lend themselves very effectively to assembly themes, especially if put into a school context: pride or vainglory; covetousness; lust; envy; gluttony; anger; sloth.

A poem, book, film, play or television programme

Take your pick! Make sure it is appropriate for your age group. You can use virtually anything to your own devices. In the past, I have used:

Poems

Poetry easily lends itself to any theme you have in mind. Have a look at: 'Not Waving But Drowning' by Stevie Smith; Hillaire Belloc's 'Cautionary Verse', a wonderful source of ideas; 'The Way Things Are' by Roger McGough; 'Footprints in the Sand' by Mary Stephenson.

Readings from books

If you're doing assembly for a whole week, it is sometimes quite refreshing for the pupils to listen to a series of excerpts from a thought-provoking book. Alternatively, you could dramatize the passages, using narrators and characters. Try these: *I am David* by Ann Holm; *The Prophet* by Khalil Gibran; *Jonathan Livingston Seagull* by Richard Bach; Jacqueline Wilson's books raise a variety of thought-provoking issues – depression, single-parent families, disability, bereavement and domestic violence to name but a few; Winnie the Pooh books lend themselves quite well to assembly themes; *Just So Stories* by Rudyard Kipling; *Alice's Adventures in Wonderland* by Lewis Carroll; The Narnia Chronicles by C.S. Lewis; The Harry Potter books by J.K. Rowling; Any book by Roald Dahl; *The Basketball Diaries* by Jim Carroll (for an older age group); La Fontaine's fables; *The Diary of Anne Frank*; *Zlata's Diary: A Child's Life in Sarajevo* by Zlata Filipovic.

Television serials/soaps

Recent developments in plots can be very useful vehicles for considering social and moral issues. There are often bulletin boards on soap opera websites, from which you can usually get the gist of what's going on without subjecting yourself to a whole episode. It seems mainly to be children and teenagers who populate these boards – so you can see what interests them. Get theme tunes from the Internet to add a bit of atmosphere.

Ongoing talent contests can be adapted. I did a one-off assembly based on *Pop Idol* – I renamed it 'Bone Idle' and did an assembly on laziness.

Game shows

Thank goodness we invented game shows! They are *the* most reliable and rich source ever. Their format is familiar and inherently entertaining to the audience. There are endless possibilities to adapt them to your own purposes. Question and answer jokes are very good for adding humour. All the following shows are perfect: *Countdown*; *Fifteen to One*; *Mastermind*; *The Weakest Link*; *Who Wants to be a Millionaire?*; *University Challenge* (you can change this to 'Universally Challenged', depending on your purposes!); *Blockbusters*; *Wheel of Fortune*; *Play Your Cards Right*.

Reality TV programmes

These are absolute gifts, especially if you're lumbered with assembly for the week. You'll have an in-built sense of continuity. All sorts of issues can be raised. It is a fresh, modern formula that has broad appeal. You can choose whether you allow the audience to vote or whether you rig it, with your own class members as the voters. Here's a few to get your juices flowing: *At Home with the Osbornes*; *Survivor*; *I'm a Celebrity Get me out of here!*; *Big Brother*; *Blind Date*; *Pop Idol/Fame Academy*.

The school's role in the community

A much-neglected matter. You could deal with: the elderly in the community; adult learning opportunities in the school. Why?; sports facilities available to others. Why?; the school and the environment.

Local clergymen, charity workers, social workers or councillors can come and visit the school and talk about their work in the community. Vet your visitors carefully: I did hear a hilarious story about a man who came into the school with his guide dog. All went well until he entered the assembly hall. Apparently, he swore like a trooper and was not averse to kicking his dog. Not quite what was called for!

A topic related to an academic subject

This could be your own specialist subject or you could pilfer from others! Memorable examples comprise:

◆ Historical anniversaries, such as the death of a monarch, peace treaties and so on.

- Classical mythology – extremely useful as there is often a moral to the story.

- Unexpected results from a scientific experiment, showing that you shouldn't take anything for granted.

- Scientific discoveries, recent or historical.

Party games and ice-breakers

These are excellent ways of demonstrating the importance of social skills such as cooperation with others. You can either set them up beforehand or ask for 'volunteers/conscripts' from the audience. With a bit of imagination, a great number of games are suitable. Here are a few that I have used in the past:

Spoonfeeding

Two pupils are given large spoons and some sweets are placed in a bowl. They are told that they are welcome to have some sweets but they can't use their hands or touch the bowl with any part of their body. It should soon become apparent that they have to put the handle of the spoon in their mouths and feed the other person like that.

Shoe find

Tell between six and ten pupils to stand in a circle, take off their right shoe and place it in the centre of the circle. Tell them that when you give the signal you want them to go into the centre of the circle and get a shoe that doesn't belong to them. They return to their place in the circle and put the shoe in their right hand. Tell them to join hands. When they have done that, tell them that they must return the shoes to their rightful owners without breaking the circle.

The blanket game

[This is more suited to an older audience] You have to set this one up beforehand. Pick a 'volunteer' (whom you have thoroughly primed and who has discreetly secreted items of clothing, including underwear, about his person!) from the audience. Tell him to sit on the floor. Place a large blanket over him. Tell him that you are thinking about *something* that you wish him to take off. You have written down the name of that thing on a piece of paper in an envelope. Show the envelope to the audience. If he manages to take off that item, you will let him come out from under the blanket. A lot of movement under the blanket should ensue and an item of clothing should appear. Start with innocuous things like a watch or tie. Towards the end, the underwear should emerge and the audience will believe that there is a naked person under the blanket. At this stage, the blanket can be lifted to reveal a fully clothed person. Tell the audience you fooled the audience because of their preconceived ideas and that they should always question what they see. You can doubly fool them by placing someone under the blanket before the audience come in.

Assemblies Made Easy

During the game, the person passes out clothing of the opposite sex (or even a teacher's clothes). I can guarantee they'll get a real shock when you raise the blanket.

I hope the above ideas have helped you on your way to divine inspiration.

3

To Pray or Not to Pray

I have already dealt with my hang-ups. If you're comfortable praying, pray away! In any case, you'll have to adhere to your school policy on prayer (there's almost bound to be one nowadays). There are alternatives. You could summarize your message and just encourage your students to reflect silently at the end. Alternatively, you could finish with a reading from a spiritual book such as *The Prophet* (this book has passages on a multitude of subjects). *Jonathan Livingston Seagull* also lends itself well to this.

4

Teacher-centred Assemblies

Checklist

◆ Keep it short.

◆ Keep it simple.

◆ Have a visual focus, if possible – make sure it's in *everyone's* line of vision.

◆ Make it age-specific and relevant.

◆ Be up front and personal.

◆ Make them laugh.

◆ Choose appropriate music to accompany your theme.

◆ Learn your material – you'll be more credible and you won't need notes.

◆ Rehearse, rehearse, rehearse. Out *loud*! With gestures and appropriate facial expressions – if you're delivering bad news, don't look as if you've just won the lottery.

Delivery

◆ Can everyone see you?

- Start off quietly to gain your audience's full attention.

- Talk slowly, but talk!

- Stand *still*!

- Make sure your body language and position in the room are not defensive – come out, we know you're there!

- Let your words trigger your actions – if you're counting, count on your fingers; if you're saying no, shake your head.

- Avoid irritating gestures – you are *not* an air traffic controller.

- Keep your head up, although an in-depth study of ceiling aesthetics is not necessary.

- Look your audience in the eyes, in a pleasant, non-threatening manner.

- Give them time to react to what you're saying – but not too much time.

Controlling your nerves

It's quite useful to understand why you're:

- having palpitations.

- sweating profusely.

- shaking.

- feeling tension in your neck and shoulders.

- talking in a ridiculously tremulous voice.

- experiencing a pressing urge to go and commune with the toilet.

- wanting to stay there for the foreseeable future.

- generally looking as if you're in the early stages of detox.

Fear of public speaking is in the top five of phobias, ranking alongside financial ruin and death! So, *don't* worry, you're anxiety is quite natural. Why?

- you're in a totally unfamiliar situation.

- you therefore lack confidence.

- you feel isolated standing alone in front of your audience.

- you're frightened of making a fool of yourself.

- you're scared your job/career may depend upon the consequences.

What can you do about them?

Before your assembly:

- go to a private place (*not* home!).

- try to relax your body by doing the exercises of your choice.

- take deep breaths.

- sing a silly song – it'll relax you and your voice. I

always go for 'I'm in the mood for dancing', by the Nolan Sisters.

◆ get to the assembly hall early, but not too early or you'll have to go back to the silly song stage.

◆ talk to anyone who is there and listen intently to what they say, however boring it may be – it'll take your mind off things.

During your assembly:

◆ don't hold notes – any trembling will be more obvious and they'll create a barrier between you and your audience.

◆ try to imagine you're just chatting to friends.

◆ lean on something if you feel your legs shaking.

◆ visualize any 'frowners/head shakers': in their underwear, naked, with a large tuberous vegetable growing out of their head, or sitting on a potty.

There is nothing wrong with being or feeling vulnerable. If anything, it will make your audience more sympathetic. Your nervousness is not as visible as you think it is.

I would be lying through my teeth if I said I had totally conquered my nerves. I haven't. However, I have learnt not to get nervous about getting nervous.

5

Two Examples of Teacher-based Assemblies

I wrote these assemblies to appeal to as broad an age range as possible (I was in a school that went from Key Stage 2 to Sixth form), and to fit into a 15-minute slot in the timetable.

You'll have to take both these factors into consideration. You can be far more risqué if your audience is older and you haven't got a priggish head teacher (*not* that I did!).

You can lead a horse to water, but you can't make it drink

Let me take you back a couple of years ago, to when I was fifteen. My family tell me that I was at my *most* argumentative at that age. Whenever I had done something wrong, my stepfather would sit me down and painstakingly try to point out the error of my ways. As a matter of principle, I would strongly disagree with everything he said. Then, I'd give him the benefit of my expert opinion on the subject in hand. After about half an hour, my stepfather would resist the temptation to strangle me, sigh, shrug his shoulders and mutter: 'You can lead a horse to water, but you can't make it drink'.

Assemblies Made Easy

I have a confession to make. I'm very ashamed to say that when Mrs Jones 'asked' me to do this assembly, my first reaction was: 'How can I get out of this?' Quite frankly, I'd rather eat a slug. My mind raced through the possible escape routes:

A few days before the assembly, I could start showing symptoms of a rather nasty bacterial virus. By the date in question, my illness would have developed into full-blown Welsh flu, B-strain. Right now, I'd be tucked up at home, watching *This Morning*, eagerly awaiting the phone-in on hamster psychology.

Perhaps I could arrange for my car to be stolen just before 8.30. Right now, I'd be helping police with their enquiries.

I briefly thought about the possibility of bribing another teacher into doing this assembly for me. How many lunch duties were equivalent to one assembly? How many marked exercise books? How many lesson supervisions? Would they accept a cheque? Visa? American Express? Organ Donor card? Or did they operate on a strictly cash-only basis? Did I have any dodgy photographs to blackmail them with? I came to realize, however, that this particular option would be out of the question. As we all know, they are fine, upstanding and incorruptible members of society.

It then occurred to me that it's quite a long time since someone asked me to do something I really didn't want to do. Then something else occurred to me. Two things in one day! That's a lot for me! What occurred to me is that you lot are often being asked to do things you don't fancy much. Ring any bells?

Does your mind ever wander in lessons? Does it

ever completely switch off from what the teacher is saying? No, of course it doesn't! Perish the thought. But, if it ever does in the future, you may find yourself wondering what your teachers were like when they were at school. Picture them, right at the front of the classroom, bolt upright in their chairs, pens poised for action and listening to every word uttered by their lovely teacher. Their homework would always be handed in on time and they would even volunteer to do extra homework, because they knew it was good for them.

No, no, no! I happen to know that many of your teachers were self-confessed disaster areas at school. I happen to know that one of them diverted all the local traffic through the school grounds using borrowed traffic cones. Another was expelled from nursery school for putting pencils through holes in the floorboards. I used to specialize in unpleasant activity avoidance. I would spend days on end planning how to avoid things like piano lessons, hockey in the rain and, of course, the dreaded homework. The excuses I used to come up with make you look like complete amateurs. However, my expert capabilities would always end up getting me into big trouble.

At the ripe old age of 21 and three quarters, I can now see that my antics didn't do me any favours. I always ended up with more problems than I'd started with. And, what about today? What if I had managed to wriggle out of doing this assembly through a rather too convenient illness, orchestrated car theft or bribery and corruption? I could now be facing any of the following consequences: the 'silent treatment' in the staffroom, lunch duty for life, a charge of wasting police time or an unauthorized overdraft. Not very nice.

Now think about the times when you get into trouble with your teachers, parents and even your friends. I should imagine that it's often when someone is trying to force you to do something you'd rather not do. Maybe they're trying to say something you don't want to hear.

Next time you're faced with this situation, I hope at least you'll consider what I've said. Probably you'll have to learn this in your own time and in your own way. Just like me. After all, 'you can lead a horse to water, but you can't make it drink'.

[This was followed by a brief reading from The Prophet *about knowledge. Then we reflected upon confronting things that we find difficult and the sense of achievement we feel when we've faced up to a challenge and overcome our difficulties.]*

A rolling stone gathers no moss

[Last time I gave an assembly, I used a proverb as my central theme. I love proverbs. In fact, I collect them. Yes, I'm that sad! At the moment, I've gathered a grand total of 108.]

The dictionary definition of a proverb is: 'A popular saying expressed in a clever, brief manner'. Proverbs are very old and have been passed down from generation to generation. I like to think that everyone of them contains a little gem of wisdom. In theory, I ought to be able to base an assembly on each of them. *Don't* tell Mrs Jones! As they're so old, many of them sound strange. For example, I wouldn't relish the prospect of talking for ten minutes about these: 'Laugh and grow fat'; 'Little pitchers have long ears'; 'A great cry and little wool'. Anyway, the next proverb on my list is: 'A rolling stone gathers no moss'.

Before I talk about stones, rolling or otherwise, I want to tell you about my problem. If I sit down during the day, I feel *guilty*. I blame my parents. They're farmers and every minute from dawn till dusk is filled with frenzied activity. When, not long ago, I was a child, my parents made it clear that to relax during the day was *not* the done thing. The *evening* was the time for relaxation. Breakfast was at eight o'clock or there was no breakfast. If we loitered around the house doing nothing, my mother would forcibly eject us. If she felt it necessary, she would lock the door behind us. Even worse, she would give us what she called 'constructive' things to do. Planting lettuces and picking blackcurrants were the worst ones.

So you can see the origins of my problem. I now have the compulsion to cram my day to the brim with as much activity as possible. If you can sit down during the day without feeling guilty, then I envy you.

Let's return to the rolling stone. 'A rolling stone gathers no moss'. This would seem to imply that if a stone is *not* rolling it *would* gather moss. Before I continue, I would like to make is quite clear that I have absolutely nothing against moss. I am *not* anti-moss. I do not adhere to the mossist philosophy. In fact, I'm very partial to a bit of moss here and there.

Picture that stone. It stays in the same place for a very long time. Nobody moves it or uses it for anything. Time passes. Moss starts to grow on it. It is no longer a moss-free stone. That poor little stone is a picture of decay and neglect.

'A *rolling* stone gathers *no* moss'. Think about what that proverb is trying to tell you. Before you start, I can assure you that it has absolutely nothing to do with Mick Jagger's gardening habits. To me, and *don't* correct me if I'm wrong, it means that it's good to be active, both physically and mentally.

Do you ever think about how wonderful it would be not to have to do anything? Imagine yourself in your own little paradise – a life dedicated to pleasure and relaxation. For me, this island of contentment has no books to mark, no lessons to prepare, no queues at the photocopier, no ironing boards, no washing up, no dentists … I could go on for days, but I've got a lesson with Year 11 and I couldn't bear to disappoint them. This island is always sunny and warm. There's an endless supply of life's essentials: beef with green peppers and black bean sauce, barbecued spare ribs, Quick Brew teabags, sherbet fountains, French bread and rare fillet steak. The waves are gently lapping onto the beach. The atmosphere is calm and soothing. Bruce Willis pops around occasionally in his apron to vacuum the beach and dust off the palm trees.

What would your island of contentment be like? It can be however you wish. The only requirement would be that you don't have to do anything. Idleness and enjoyment are compulsory on this island.

Alternatively, think about how different school would be if you didn't have to do anything. One rainy Monday morning, such as this one, you've got eight tests and a quadruple session of your worst subject. Mr Thomas enters the school for assembly and says: 'I'm sorry, there's been a terrible mistake. We've got it all wrong. The teachers and I would like to take this opportunity to apologise to all pupils for all the tedious and time-consuming lessons and homework we've given you in the past.' The new school motto is *Labora est*, 'work is unnecessary'. He then outlines the new school curriculum. Here are the details of a few subjects: I'll start with French, as that is the most important subject. French is a round the clock extravaganza of 'Lotto'. Real money is staked and everyone wins because you can cheat if you want to. French is followed by geography, in which you are given a map with directions to your favourite shopping centre. In maths you're given some spending money to count. Latin is a non-stop toga party, hosted by Mr Williams – no change there then! And, well, history is history!

Publicity experts would flood to the school with a ready-made marketing strategy. They would only have to make minor changes to famous advertising slogans:

- 'Happiness is a school called [...].'

- '[...] – eight out of ten pupil owners who expressed a preference said their child preferred it.'

- '[...] – the school that likes to say: "*Yes!*" (but only if you want it to).'

- 'New [...] Power biologically removes all that hard-to-shift print that others leave behind. Gives your textbooks, timetables and reports that special bluey whiteness.'

You may think I've come a long way from rolling stones. However, think long enough and deeply enough about any situation in which you don't *have* to do anything. Eventually, you will conclude that you would be bored. Very bored. There would be no reason at all for getting up in the morning. Your days would become empty. You would be like that poor, dejected, moss-gathering stone. Boredom is at best a bad thing and, at worst, dangerous. Boredom leads people to do things that they would *never* do if they led fulfilling and active lives.

A combination of intellectual stimulation and physical exercise is *vitally* important if we are to live life to the full. Mr Williams, a superb sportsman and a fine classical scholar, is living (just!) proof of this.

Whether you're a stone or not, intellectual stimulation is essential in order to avoid the encroachment of the dreaded moss. I'm not only talking about schoolwork. After all: 'Too much work makes Jack a dull boy,' as another proverb goes. No, I'm thinking about interests you may have: music, art, trainspotting, the history of anoraks, pedigree woodlouse breeding – absolutely *anything*! Having interests makes you a more *interesting* person. It means that when you've finished your schoolwork, you don't turn into an utter blob! That's brutal, I know, but let's face it: if you're bored, you're probably pretty boring too.

Physical exercise is also important. I am convinced that the reason some of you find it difficult to sit still in lessons is that you're simply too full of energy to sit down. There I am, attempting to pass on the joys of the perfect tense or campsite French, and you would much rather be running around outside. And, why not? What if you had been running around beforehand? A good vigorous cross-country scamper (five miles perhaps?) before the intellectual delights of lessons? An *excellent* idea! Afterwards, you'd be nicely sedated and your little grey cells would be poised and ready for action. What is more, some of you wouldn't look and feel as if you need oxygen or emergency resuscitation upon reaching the first floor!

Remember that page at the end of your reports that you have to complete? You record the details of your extra-curricular activities and achievements. Some of you have wide-ranging interests and find it difficult to fit them all on the page. Think of people in your year who are like that. Think of them as 'moss-free stones'. They are never bored. They are the ones who are interested and enthusiastic. As a result, they are interesting and inspire enthusiasm in others. Not only are they more likely to be successful, but, far more importantly, they are more likely to be happy and fulfilled. Are you like that? Or are you this person: you struggle for hours to fill in that page on your report; eventually, you come up with 'watching television' or 'recreational breathing'. Do you experience emotional trauma and/or a severe physical reaction if you miss your favourite television programme or someone dares to suggest you do something to help around the house? Are you a 'moss-prone stone'?

[I ended with another reading from The Prophet *about work. A reflection on the importance of leading life to the full followed.]*

6

The Class Act: Examples of Class Assemblies

Much of the advice given for teacher-centred assemblies applies to class-based assemblies as well. Doing an assembly with your class can be a great bonding experience, providing you involve *everybody* from the outset. As far as possible, let them naturally fall into the role with which they feel most comfortable – making props, looking after the scripts and so on. Try to ensure *everyone* has a speaking part.

Class sizes vary enormously, so I've bullet-pointed the parts wherever feasible. I have kept stage directions to a minimum, because I have no idea where these assemblies will be performed. I haven't made extensive lists of props because it's up to you how elaborate you make your performance. My advice is to keep them to a minimum – if it can go wrong, it will do!

Racism

This assembly can be done at any time during the school year. However, the second Sunday of September is 'Racial Justice Sunday', which aims to make people more aware of the issues surrounding racial justice.

Cast

MARTIN LUTHER KING
NARRATOR
Up to 13 other pupils

[MARTIN LUTHER KING *is sitting at a desk writing in a prison cell*]

- 'Injustice anywhere is a threat to justice everywhere.'

- Let us go back in time to 1963. We are in the United States of America.

- Dr Martin Luther King, a campaigner for racial equality, is in jail in Birmingham, Alabama.

- On 16th April, from his prison cell, Martin Luther King wrote:

NARRATOR I am in Birmingham because injustice is here. We have waited for more than 340 years for our constitutional and God-given rights. The nations of Asia and Africa are moving with jet-like speed towards gaining political independence, but we still creep at horse-and-buggy pace toward getting a cup of coffee at a lunch counter. Perhaps it is easy for those who have never felt the stinging dark of segregation to say,

- 'Wait.'

NARRATOR But when you have seen vicious mobs lynch your mothers and fathers at will and drown your sisters and brothers at whim; when you have seen hate-filled policemen curse, kick and even kill your black brothers and sisters: when you see the vast majority of your twenty million Negro brothers smothering in an air-tight cage of poverty in the midst of an affluent society; when you suddenly find your tongue twisted and your speech stammering as you seek to explain to your six-year-old daughter why she can't go to the public amusement park that has just been advertised on television, and see tears welling up in her eyes when she is told that Funtown is closed to coloured children, and see ominous clouds of inferiority beginning to form in her little mental sky, and see her beginning to distort her personality by developing an unconscious bitterness toward white people; when you have to concoct an answer to your five-year-old son who is asking:

- 'Daddy, why do white people treat coloured people so mean?';

NARRATOR When you take a cross-country drive and find it necessary to sleep night after night in the uncomfortable corners of your automobile because no motel will accept you; when you are humiliated day in and day out by nagging signs reading 'white' and 'coloured'; when your first name becomes 'nigger', your middle name becomes 'boy' (however old you are) and your last name becomes 'John', and your wife and mother are never given the respected title 'Mrs'; when you are harried by day and haunted by night by the fact that you are a Negro, living constantly at tiptoe stance, never quite knowing what to expect next, and are plagued with inner fears and outer resentments; when you know forever fighting a degenerating 'nobodiness' then you will understand why we find it difficult to wait.

- Martin Luther King was in jail because he was protesting about racial injustice.

- How much do you think the world has changed?

[*At this point recent press cuttings could be used to*

47

illustrate examples of racial injustice and their conse-quences. The issues of racial violence and the plight of refugees and asylum seekers could be raised]

◆ It is important that we remember that racial injustice is not only about statistics and sensationalist press cover-age.

◆ It is about real people and how they are treated.

◆ And how we treat each other.

◆ Baroness Amos, who represented Britain at a con-ference in South Africa said:

◆ 'The multicultural nature of British society is one of the first things you notice when you arrive in the UK. Our culture is born of the talents and creativity of many different groups – White, Black, Asian and other minorities. In London alone, nearly 200 languages other than English are spoken. A quarter of London's school pupils speak a language other than English at home. Racism is a reality that affects us all. It manifests itself in different ways, in different parts of the world. It can be direct or indirect, individual or institutional.'

Girl Power: an assembly to mark International Women's Day

Cast
Up to 25 pupils

◆ What do you do if your dishwasher breaks down?

◆ Divorce her.

◆ What does it mean if your wife serves you breakfast in bed?

48

- The chain is too long.

- Why haven't they sent many women to the moon?

- Because it doesn't need cleaning yet.

- Behind these jokes we want to bring you a serious message.

- Many women all over the world are victims of exploitation and discrimination.

- Every single minute a woman dies in childbirth.

- Women are more at risk from HIV infection than men.

- HIV-infected women in Africa now outnumber HIV-infected men by a massive two million.

- As many women die from violence as from cancer.

- One woman in three will experience violence during her lifetime.

- 60 per cent of the world's poor are women.

- Two thirds of illiterate people are women.

- 350 million women do not have access to contraception.

- Only one woman in eight has a political franchise.

- Despite the fact that girls outperform boys at school, their earning power is significantly less than that of boys.

- Today, to mark International Women's Day, we wish to celebrate the achievements of women who have overcome adversity, prejudice and difficulty.

- They have learnt how to lead.

- They use their gifts to their full potential.

◆ They are equal partners in endeavouring to make this world a better place.

[*At this stage, you could either outline the lives of some outstanding women or ask pupils to make brief presentations about women they admire, famous or unknown, contemporary or historical. For example, a local business woman, nurse, social worker, relation, Ellen Macarthur, Evelyn Glennie, Paula Radcliffe, Emma Richards, J.K. Rowling, Rosa Parks, Mother Theresa, Queen Elizabeth I, Joan of Arc, Elizabeth Fry, Edith Cavell, Florence Nightingale, Beatrix Potter . . .*]

◆ Women had an important part to play in the Christian story.

◆ Mary was chosen to be his mother.

◆ And it was women who discovered that he had risen from the dead.

[*You could follow this with readings from the Bible – Luke 1:28–33, Matthew 28:1, 5–8*]

The Hindu festival Of Divali

[*This Hindu festival is celebrated in November but the assembly can be performed at any time of the year to symbolize the triumph of good over evil, or light over darkness. You could also make links with other religions' festivals in which light and hope play an important part (Hanukah and Christmas, for example)*]

Cast

RAMA	FAWN
SITA	HANUMAN
RAVANA	VARIOUS ANIMALS
Up to 12 other pupils	

50

Props
Divali lights/tea lights

[*To make Divali lamps: Take some plasticine, salt dough or clay. Form an oval shape with a flat bottom and stick a candle or night light in one end. Leave to harden if necessary. More elaborate versions can be made if time allows*]

NARRATOR Long ago, in India, there lived a good king called Rama.

[*Enter Rama*]

RAMA I am a good king called Rama.
NARRATOR Rama had a beautiful wife called Sita.

[*Enter Sita*]

SITA Does my bum look big in this?
RAMA What bum, my sweet?
NARRATOR They lived in a forest and made friends with all the animals.

[*Enter a selection of ANIMALS with whom RAMA and SITA shake hands. The ANIMALS sit down*]

NARRATOR All was well until Ravana, the demon king, came along. He was struck by Sita's beauty.

[*Enter RAVANA. The animals flinch*]

RAVANA Haven't I seen you somewhere before?
SITA Yes, that's why I don't go there anymore.
RAVANA I would go to the ends of the earth for you.
SITA Yes, but would you stay there?
RAVANA Your place or mine?
SITA Both. You go to yours and I'll go to mine.
NARRATOR Ravana realized that his boyish charms did not seem to be having the desired effect. So, knowing that Sita was an animal lover, he conjured up a fawn.

51

[*Enter a FAWN. SITA is captivated.*]

SITA What a lovely fawn!

[*The FAWN runs off stage. Exit all the ANIMALS*]

SITA Rama! The fawn has gorn! Where can it be?
RAMA No idea, deer.
SITA Fallow that fawn!

[*Exit RAMA, chasing the FAWN*]

NARRATOR Rama chased the fawn but was soon lost in the forest. Ravana seized his opportunity and took Sita off to his castle.

[*Exit RAVANA and SITA*]

NARRATOR When Rama returned, he was horrified to see that Sita had disappeared.

[*Enter RAMA*]

RAMA Hi honey! I'm home! Oh no! Where is she?
NARRATOR Hanuman, the king of the monkeys, said he would help.

[*Enter HANUMAN*]

HANUMAN I'll help!

[*Exit HANUMAN and RAMA*]

NARRATOR Rama gathered his army of animals and headed for Ravana's castle. Hanuman went to see Sita and told her she'd soon be safe.
HANUMAN [*from offstage*] You'll soon be safe.

[*Enter RAVANA, followed by RAMA and the ANIMALS.*]

RAVANA Oh look! A travelling circus! You don't stand a chance!
RAMA Good will triumph over evil.

RAVANA So where are your armies?
RAMA Up my sleevies!

[*Enter some* PARROTS *who attack* RAVANA *and defeat him. Exit* RAVANA. *Enter* SITA *who embraces* RAMA. RAMA *shakes hands with the* PARROTS *to thank them*]

RAMA Thank goodness for the parrotroopers! You deserve a slap up meal.

[*He hands the* PARROTS *some Pollyfilla. They exit*]

SITA Polygon!

[*Exit* RAMA *and* SITA *and all the* ANIMALS]

NARRATOR Rama and Sita returned to their kingdom. Good had triumphed over evil. When they got home it was very late and so it was really dark. All the people put little lights in their home so that Rama and Sita could find their way home.

[*Enter whole class, carrying divas*]

◆ These little lights are called divas.

◆ There is a festival called Divali.

◆ Divali is a festival of lights.

◆ It lasts between three and five days.

◆ Divali means 'cluster of lights'.

◆ It is celebrated by Hindus and Sikhs.

◆ The story of Rama and Sita is told at Divali.

◆ It is the story of good triumphing over evil, light over darkness.

◆ Places can be dark, but our lives can also feel dark when we are sad or frightened.

- When good things happen in our lives, we feel brighter, as if a light has been turned on.

- For many people, Divali is also the beginning of a new year.

- It's a time for plans, new starts and hope.

Always look on the bright side of life

Cast

POSITIVE	BEYOND HOPE
NEGATIVE	Up to 20 other pupils

Props

Glass of coloured drink	Mobile phone
Tape recorder	Pen
Recording of 'Always look	Camera
on the bright side of life'	Fly swat
(cut out the naughty bits!)	Rubber bands

[*Play 'Always look on the bright side of life' as pupils enter*]

- Good morning. Welcome to Year 8 assembly.

[*if sunny*]

- And what a lovely day it is too.

[*if raining*]

- And what a lovely day it is too. It may be raining, but I'm sure the sun will come out later.

- We may have quadruple Maths, BCG injections and dead sheep stew for lunch today, but I'm sure it'll be a fun-filled, formative and fascinating day. The time will fly by and, before we know it, it will be time to go home.

54

ALL Hurray!

- Our theme today is: 'Think positive'.

- In almost every situation we face, there is a positive side ...

> [*Enter POSITIVE, looking happy*]

- and a negative side.

> [*Enter NEGATIVE, looking miserable*]

- Some people are naturally optimistic.

> [*POSITIVE stands forward and points at half a glass of drink, placed prominently on the stage*]

POSITIVE That glass is half full.

- Some people are naturally pessimistic.

> [*NEGATIVE stands forward and points at the glass*]

NEGATIVE That glass is half empty.

- And, sadly, some people are beyond hope.

> [*Enter BEYOND HOPE, who points at the glass.*]

BEYOND HOPE That glass is cracked!

- However bad a problem may seem, there is usually a positive way of looking at it.

> [*POSITIVE looks smug. NEGATIVE looks sulky. BEYOND HOPE walks off*]

- In the words of the twentieth-century icon and philosopher,

- David Essex,

- 'Every cloud has a silver lining'.

◆ For example, here we all are on [*insert date*]. End of year exams are looming on the horizon.

POSITIVE I can only do my best. At least it will be the summer holidays soon.
NEGATIVE I'm going to fail!

◆ Imagine you've just split up with the love of your life.

POSITIVE Oh well. It wasn't meant to be. There are plenty more fish in the sea.
NEGATIVE I can't live without him!

◆ Remember the old cliché, you wait for a bus for an hour and then three come along?

NEGATIVE Why do they always come in threes?
POSITIVE Oh good, I get to choose!

◆ Imagine another scenario. You are trapped in a lift.

NEGATIVE Oh no! I'll never get out of here alive!
POSITIVE Brilliant! I've always wanted to be trapped in a lift!
ALL Why?

[*Lights out. A group of pupils arrange themselves on the stage, as if they are trapped in a lift. They mime the activities that POSITIVE is about to describe. Lights on*]

POSITIVE I've always wanted to try out my being-trapped-in-a-lift tricks and I'd have a captive audience.

◆ What would you do?

POSITIVE I'd call the Psychic Hotline from my mobile and ask if they know which floor I'm on; swat at flies that didn't exist; shoot rubber bands at everyone; bring a camera and take pictures of everyone, and stand in the corner reading a phone book and laughing uproariously.

◆ You're always laughing.

[Lights out. Pupils regroup for final section]

- Recent research in gelatology, the science of laughter, has shown that laughter is an all-round healthy sport.

- A sort of internal jogging.

- Twenty seconds of laughter is equivalent to three minutes of rowing.

- A smile increases the face value of a person.

- Medically and biologically, a smile is healthy.

- It only requires 12 facial muscles to smile and 15 to laugh. Frowning uses 113 facial muscles.

- Laughter is the best medicine.

- Here are the physiological benefits of laughter.

- It reduces the levels of stress hormones,

- Which boosts the immune system.

- It lessens blood pressure and heart rate.

- It clears the respiratory tract.

- It gives the muscles in your diaphragm, face, back and respiratory system a workout.

- Psychologically, laughter lifts us up out of our pool of problems and allows us to gain a new insight.

- A shared joke gives us a sense of belonging.

- We are in control whether we know it or not.

- We can be positive or negative,

- enthusiastic or dull,

- active or passive.

- Abraham Lincoln said: 'Most folks are about as happy as they make up their minds to be'.

- This is not a rehearsal.

- This is life.

- Enjoy!

[*A reflection on the importance of living life to the full follows. Play 'Always look on the bright side of life' as pupils exit*]

Don't judge by appearances

Cast
CONTESTANT 1: stereotypically French
CONTESTANT 2: stereotypically dumb blond
CONTESTANT 3: stereotypically local, speaks with an exaggeratedly thick accent.
CILLA BLACK
LEONARD: not the sharpest knife in the drawer
Up to 27 other pupils

- Welcome to Year 9 assembly.

- For the first time in living memory, our school is establishing a school council A (general, council) election is about to take place.

- Every pupil in this school will be allowed to vote for a class representative/Everyone over the age of 18 will be able to choose a politician to represent them, providing they have UK citizenship and are not in prison.

- In selecting our representatives, we'll have to make choices and judgements about other people.

- Following the elections, we will have to accept the consequences of our choices and judgements.

- Almost every minute of every day, we have to make judgements about other people.

- Often, our judgements are based on

- The way they speak,

- The way they look,

- The way they walk,

- The way they behave,

- The car they drive,

- Where they live

- And even the football team they support.

- To illustrate the issues of judgements, choices and consequences, Year 9 productions PLC brings you two live, exclusive editions of *Blind Date*.

[Lights out. Lights on]

CILLA Good evening chooks, and welcome to this week's *Blind Date*. We're gonna have a lorra lorra laughs. Let's go and meet the contestants. What's your name and where do you come from?

CONTESTANT 1 Er ... bonjour. Bof! Papa ... Nicole. Je m'appelle Marie-Claire et j'habite en France. I eat zee smelly cheese.

CILLA Ooh er. Hiya Marie-*Cler* from *Cler*-mont Ferrand on Fronts. And where's la Fronts, Marie-*Cler*?

CONTESTANT 1 Ce n'est pas la Fronts, c'est la France.

CILLA Alright, *Cler*, keep yer *er* on. Auf Wiedersehen, pet.

CONTESTANT 1 Hein?

CILLA And now for gorgeous Contestant Number Two. What's your name and where do you come from?

CONTESTANT 2 My name's Barbie. I have one brain cell – as

a blond, that makes me 'gifted' – and I live in this big ...
er ... house thing. You know, with a roof and windows
and a little door thing ... with a Porsche outside.

CILLA So you're a bit Porsche, are you chook?

CONTESTANT 2 No, Wesley gave it to me to celebrate our
time together.

CILLA Which anniversary was it?

[*CONTESTANT 2 counts on fingers*]

CONTESTANT 2 Three days.

CILLA Was it the wheel thing?

CONTESTANT 2 No. I got tyred of him. He drove me crazy
and the car clashed with his hair.

CILLA Clashed with his *er*? I'm gobsmacked. Well, chook,
let's hope we can steer you in the right direction tonight
along the highway of happiness. And on to Contestant
Number Three. What's your name and where do you
come from?

CONTESTANT 3 I'm Irene. And I'm from round here [*insert
the name of a place that is generally looked down on in
your area*], to be precise.

[*CILLA looks at her as if she's something
that's been trodden into her favourite shagpile*]

CILLA Now that we've met all the contestants, let's go over
to the lucky lad who has to choose between these three
lovely ladies. Hello, chook, what's your name and where
do you come from?

LEONARD My name's Leonard and I live with my Mum. She
cooks my dinner.

CILLA So what do you like to eat, *Ler*-ned ?

LEONARD Er ... well, mainly food.

CILLA So fire away with your question, *Ler*-ned.

LEONARD Hello girls.

CONTESTANTS Hiya, *Ler*-ned.

LEONARD I wanna know what you like doing after your dinner. And this one goes to Contessa Number One.

CONTESTANT 1 Je ne comprends pas.

LEONARD Phwoar ... a Swede. I love swede for my dinner. Contessa Number Two?

CONTESTANT 2 Dinner? I let him pay ... you know ... the ... er ... bill – that piece of paper you get for free after the latte.

LEONARD That's cool babe. Contessa Number ... Five.

CILLA Sorry, chook, there's only three.

LEONARD Right ... er ... Contessa Number ... next one then.

CONTESTANT 3 Can't remember the question.

LEONARD Me neither.

[*Lights out. Exit* LEONARD. *Lights on*]

◆ As you may have noticed, we have selected and genetically modified our characters very carefully. We had a French person, a blond and a local person for local people ... or at least, that's what you thought they were.

◆ They were instantly recognizable, because they were stereotypes.

◆ Marie-Claire is, in fact, from Glasgow.

◆ Our blond is a brain surgeon.

◆ Our [*insert name of place*] resident is the Queen's corgi assistant, and lives in Windsor.

◆ Leonard can't join us because he's flown back to NASA.

◆ And, Cilla isn't really Cilla.

[*Everyone gasps in horror*]

◆ So, appearances can be deceptive.

- We hoped to make you question the way you judge other people.

- As the famous Native American saying goes: 'Never judge a man until you've walked a mile in his moccasins.'

- As Antoine de Saint-Exupéry said: 'L'essentiel est invisible aux yeux.'

- What is essential is invisible to the eyes.

[*Follow this with a reflection on the theme of the assembly. Ask one of your pupils to write it*]

A light-hearted look at school rules

Cast

MISS TAKE	LAZY PUPIL
MISS BEHAVIOUR	DISORGANIZED PUPIL
MISS CHIEF	LATE PUPIL
UNTIDY PUPIL	Up to 29 other pupils

Props

A very messy school bag, containing a blackish banana.

[*Ask a colleague to introduce the assembly on your behalf. Rows of empty chairs should be placed on the stage. Your pupils should initially be sitting at the very front of the audience. As they say their lines, they come and sit on the chairs on the stage*]

COLLEAGUE Good morning everybody.
SCHOOL Good morning, Mr(s) [*insert name*].
COLLEAGUE This morning, Year 9 are going to take assembly.

- What assembly?

- [*insert your name*] didn't tell us.

- Typical.

- I've done it but I haven't got the sheet with me.

- Our dog ate mine.

- My brother ate mine.

- I don't think we should have to do assembly anyway.

ALL Yeah.

- I've bought a note in from my mum.

- I thought assembly was next week.

- [*looking in pockets*] It's here somewhere.

- [*yawning*] Is it home time?

- I can't be bothered to get it out of my bag.

- I'm a septic anyway.

- Don't you mean a sceptic?

- [*faces audience*] Er ... hello ... and welcome to Year 9 assembly. Actually, it's not Year 9 assembly. We just don't have the time, energy or inclination to be bothered with such matters. All that research, note-taking, preparation and, let's face it, *effort*. [*Rest of class look totally baffled by such a concept*]. It's just not our thing. Instead, we've employed three freelance assembly artistes to take the strain.

[*Enter three pupils dressed as teachers*]

- Let us introduce you to, Miss Take ...

MISS TAKE Good morning everyone.
SCHOOL Good morning, Miss Take.

Assemblies Made Easy

◆ Miss Behaviour ...

MISS BEHAVIOUR Good morning everyone.
SCHOOL Good morning, Miss Behaviour.

◆ And finally, Miss Chief.

MISS CHIEF Yo!
SCHOOL Yo, Miss Chief.

◆ Sadly, Miss Ingyoualready can't be with us this morning.
She can't be bothered to get out of bed and later she's
going shopping.

> [*All three teachers shake their heads in
> disapproval and make tutting noises*]

MISS TAKE This takes us neatly to our theme for this
morning: sloth.
MISS BEHAVIOUR Sadly, for those biology enthusiasts among
us, by 'sloth' we do not mean the long-haired, slow
moving arboreal mammal that inhabits the South
American continent.
MISS CHIEF No, no, no! Sloth has more to do with the
coloured and gel haired, slow moving [*insert name of
school*] pupil that inhabits this very building.
MISS TAKE One of the seven deadly sins, 'sloth' is defined as
...
MISS BEHAVIOUR A noun, meaning ...
MISS CHIEF Laziness,
MISS TAKE Or indolence.
MISS BEHAVIOUR However, with the scientific precision that
characterizes professionals such as ourselves, we have
isolated four main symptoms, all too commonly
[*shaking finger*] manifested by the [*insert name of
school*] pupil.
MISS CHIEF Untidiness [*points to UNTIDY PUPIL*],
MISS TAKE Laziness [*points to LAZY PUPIL*],

MISS BEHAVIOUR Disorganization [*points to DISORGANIZED PUPIL*],

MISS TAKE And lateness [*points to empty chair*].

MISS CHIEF In common with our colleagues [*gestures to teachers and winks at them*], we want assemblies to be life-changing,

MISS TAKE Earth-shattering,

MISS BEHAVIOUR And, above all,

MISS CHIEF Ed-u-cat-ion-al

MISS TAKE Experiences.

MISS BEHAVIOUR The word education, as we all know, is derived from the Latin word.

MISS CHIEF 'Ed-u-ce-re',

MISS TAKE Meaning 'to lead out of'.

MISS BEHAVIOUR We hope to lead you out of

MISS CHIEF Un-ti-di-ness [*points to UNTIDY PUPIL*]

MISS BEHAVIOUR And out of

MISS CHIEF La-zi-ness [*points to LAZY PUPIL*]

MISS BEHAVIOUR And out of

MISS CHIEF Dis-or-ga-ni-za-tion [*points to DISORGANIZED PUPIL*]

MISS BEHAVIOUR And out of

MISS CHIEF Late-ness [*points to empty chair*]

MISS TAKE We hope to create a scholastic community of tidy, punctual, dynamic and thrusting individuals.

ALL THREE TEACHERS Wicked!

ALL THREE TEACHERS

>Listen now to our verse,
>For the untidy, late and lazy.
>They do not pull their weight,
>They drive their teachers crazy.

MISS BEHAVIOUR [*to LAZY PUPIL*] [*insert name*], where's your homework, dear?

LAZY PUPIL I cannot seem to find it here.
>Alas, alack, oh woe is me,
>I did not do my history.

Assemblies Made Easy

MISS BEHAVIOUR It was late last week as well.
LAZY PUPIL Oh hush now Miss, please don't yell.
MISS CHIEF [to UNTIDY PUPIL] [insert name] tuck your shirt
    in!
UNTIDY PUPIL Do I have to Miss? My hands are hurting.
MISS CHIEF Do it now, make me happy,
    Don't roll it up! Make it snappy!
MISS BEHAVIOUR [to LAZY PUPIL] Off you go to fun P.E.
LAZY PUPIL Oh dear I have no kit with me.
    I have a note from my mummy
WHOLE CLASS It says she has a runny tummy!
MISS CHIEF [to UNTIDY PUPIL]
    Is that lipstick round your buccal cavity?
    How could you sink to such depravity?
LAZY PUPIL Sorry, Miss, now do keep calm,
    My mother says I must use balm.
MISS CHIEF I believe that that's long-lash mascara
LAZY PUPIL Oh now, Miss C, you're going too fara.
MISS TAKE [to DISORGANIZED PUPIL]
    Come by 'ere my angel
    From your bag doth come a smell.
DISORGANIZED PUPIL
    I think you'll find that it's a banana,
    All the way from French Guyana.
    It got squashed within my file,
    I think it's been there for a while.
MISS TAKE
    Rotting fruit is quite obscene,
    Your school bag should be squeaky clean.

[LATE PUPIL rushes in]

MISS TAKE Oh [insert name], late again!
LATE PUPIL What a fuss, it's only ten!
    Sorry, Miss., I missed the bus,
    And I do not give a ...

WHOLE CLASS Tinker's cuss!

[All three teachers turn to face the audience]

MISS TAKE Please don't be late, untidy, lazy,
You're wasting time – don't be crazy!

MISS BEHAVIOUR
The teachers want to help you learn,
To pass exams and earn, earn, earn!

MISS CHIEF You must work hard in every lesson,
As our head teacher's always stressing.

MISS TAKE You'll get from life what you put in
And sloth is such a deadly sin.

MISS BEHAVIOUR By the horns, seize the bull,
Live each moment to the full.

MISS CHIEF Seize the day, savour the minute,
Take your sloth and go and bin it.

*[Teachers turn to pupils who come and kneel
in gratitude in front of them]*

- Oh Miss Take

- Oh Miss Chief

- You are so right

- We are feeling so contrite.

- We believe you, Miss Behaviour

- You lovely teacher

- You utter saviour.

- Although we're feeling weak and trembly

- We'll go and write our own assembly.

Laziness/sloth

Cast

GAME SHOW HOST
CONTESTANT 1
CONTESTANT 2

JUDGE
Up to 15 other pupils

Props

Recording of 'Lazy' or 'We're busy doing nothing'.
A large sign with the word 'idle' written on it.
Two school bags, containing, amongst other things,
English dictionaries.
A fan.
A torch.
A cold compress.

[*As the school enters the assembly hall, get the pupils to sing along with a recording of 'We're busy doing nothing'. If they are reluctant to sing, even at gunpoint, play 'Lazy'*]

- Idle, adjective [*hold up sign with word 'idle' written*]

- Not employed.

- Doing nothing.

- Useless.

- Not occupied.

- Unfruitful.

- Unprofitable.

- Of no use or importance.

- For your delectation, Year 8 are proud to present the grand final of our nationwide competition to find the laziest person in Britain.

- Yes, ladies and gentlemen, from the thousands of

contestants, we're now down to the final two: [*insert first name*] totally relaxed [*insert family name*] and [*insert first name*] anymore laid back and s/he'd be horizontal [*insert family name*].

♦ Please welcome our presenter, the amazing [*insert name*].

[*All clap, and encourage audience to do the same*]

HOST Hello and welcome to 'Bone Idle 2004'. Round One is the proverbs round. Question one. If a jobs worth doing, it's worth …

CONTESTANT 1 Getting someone else to do it.

HOST If at first, you don't succeed …

CONTESTANT 2 Give up.

HOST An excellent start. Right, Round Two. Our amazing 'Bone Idle Challenge'. Contestants, listen up! You are in an English lesson [*CONTESTANTS clutch heads in horror*], and you can't remember how to spell a word. Mr(s) [*insert name of English teacher*] has made the outrageous suggestion that you look it up in a dictionary.

[*Audience and CONTESTANTS clutch their heads in horror*]

HOST This mammoth task means that you will have to: 1. Open your bag.

[*Audience and CONTESTANTS gasp in horror. A pupil comes on and fans the CONTESTANTS, who are in obvious distress*]

HOST 2. Look for your dictionary.

[*Audience and CONTESTANTS gasp in horror. A pupil comes on and checks their pulses*]

HOST 3. Open it.

> [*Audience and* CONTESTANTS *gasp in horror. A pupil comes on and shines a torch into the* CONTESTANTS' *eyes*]

HOST 4. Find the word.

> [*Audience and* CONTESTANTS *gasp in horror. A pupil enters and applies a cold compress to the* CONTESTANTS' *foreheads*]

HOST 5. Write it down.

> [*Audience and* CONTESTANTS *gasp in horror. Three pupils enter and administer first aid*]

HOST We're ready to go. You have 30 seconds.

> [*The drums roll.* CONTESTANTS *attempt each stage of the dictionary challenge but can't do it. To add a bit of humour, when they're looking in their bags, unusual objects could emerge. They could also really struggle to lift and open their dictionaries*]

HOST Stop! Your time is up! Now, over to our judge, Nasty [*insert name, preferably beginning with 'n'*], who will give her views on tonight's performances.

JUDGE These two 'people' make a slug look positively dynamic and thrusting. They have the motivation and energy of an amoeba. You only get out of life what you're prepared to put in. Unless they're prepared to put some effort into life, they'll grow up to be a waste of space and a drain on world oxygen supplies.

[*Audience claps*]

HOST Thank you, Nasty [*insert name*]. Ladies and gentle-men, the time has come. It's your chance to vote. Who do you think deserves the title of 'Bone Idle 2004'? [*insert name*] totally relaxed [*insert name*] or [*insert name*] any more laid back and she'd be horizontal [*insert name*]? Let's have a show of hands for [*insert name*]

[*Audience votes*]

HOST And [*insert name*].

[*Audience votes*]

HOST Ladies and gentlemen. 'Bone Idle 2004' is [*insert name*].

[*Audience claps*]

JUDGE Ladies and gentlemen, you only live once. Life is not a rehearsal. Carpe diem! Seize the day! Whatever opportunities you're given today, grab them!

Respect for others

Cast
ANNE ROBINSON
BACKGROUND VOICE 1
BACKGROUND VOICE 2

8 CONTESTANTS
Up to 6 other pupils

- Good morning, and welcome to Year 8's assembly.
- Our theme this morning is
- *Non sibi, sed omnibus*
- Not for oneself, but for all.
- To illustrate the importance of putting others before yourself
- Year 8 now present an exclusive edition of 'The Weakest Link'.

[*In Anne Robinson voice*] Goodbye!

ANNE Good morning and welcome to *The Weakest Link*. There are eight people here, and up to £10,000 can be won. Only one person here can leave with the money.

The others will leave with nothing. Why? Because they will have been voted off as the weakest link. It's as simple as that. Right, start the clock! [*insert name*], why didn't the chicken cross the road?

CONTESTANT 1 Because it had gone into a Korma.

ANNE Eggsactly right. [*insert name*], name two days of the week beginning with 't'.

CONTESTANT 2 Er ... today and tomorrow?

ANNE No, Tuesday and Thursday. [*insert name*],

CONTESTANT 3 Bank!

ANNE [*insert name*], what do you know about the Dead Sea?

CONTESTANT 3 I didn't even know it was ill.

ANNE It's an inland island sea of 160,000 square miles between south-east Europe and Asia, connected to the Aegean Sea by the Bosphorus, the sea of Marmora, and the Dardanelles and to the sea of Aziv by the Kerch Strait. [*insert name*], what's an archaeologist?

CONTESTANT 4 A person whose career lies in ruins?

ANNE Correct! [*insert name*] Why shouldn't you try to swim on a full stomach?

CONTESTANT 5 Because it's easier to swim on a full swimming pool?

ANNE No. Because it can lead to muscular cramps, drowning and death. Name two pronouns.

CONTESTANT 6 Who? Me?

ANNE Correct! [*insert name*], what does 'depend' mean?

CONTESTANT 7 The end of the swimming pool with most water?

ANNE No! To put trust in, rely on, be sure of, influenced by, resultant from, to be undecided or pending. From the Latin 'dependere' to hang from. [*insert name*], define the word 'elliptical'.

CONTESTANT 8 Er ... a kiss from a man with a moustache?

ANNE No! It means relating to or having the shape of an

ellipse, which is a closed conic section shaped like a flattened circle and formed by an inclined plane that does not cut the base of the cone. Where x squared over a squared plus y squared over b squared, assuming 2a and 2b are the lengths of the minor axes. Area equals pi a b. [*insert Contestant 1's name*], complete this quotation from the Bible. 'It came to ...'

CONTESTANT 1 Pass.

ANNE Correct! [*insert Contestant 2's name*], what do you call a route through a range of mountaiuns where there is a gap between peaks?

CONTESTANT 2 Pass!

ANNE Correct! [*insert Contestant 4's name*], in sport, what do you call the transfer of a ball from one player to another?

CONTESTANT 4 Pass!

ANNE Correct! [*insert Contestant 3's name*], *The Wind in the Willows* is also known as *Tales from the River* ...

CONTESTANT 3 Bank!

ANNE Correct! [*insert Contestant 5's name*], in music ...

[*The buzzer sounds to signal the end of the round*]

ANNE Time's up! I cannot finish the question. Well, team, you have won a measly £20 out of a possible £10,000. Hardly MENSA material, are you! DENSA, more like! You make a breezeblock look like a superior life form! It's time to vote off who you think is the weakest link!

BACKGROUND VOICE 1 Stotastically ... stitostically, statistically ..., [*insert Contestant 3's name*], is the strongest link, because s/he banked the most money.

BACKGROUND VOICE 2 Although, [*insert names of Contestants 1, 4 and 6*] did answer their questions correctly. But will the votes follow the facts?

ANNE Right! Pens down! Voting over! It's time to reveal who you think is the weakest link.

Assemblies Made Easy

[The CONTESTANTS write down their choices. In turn the pupils show their cards]

CONTESTANT 1 Nobody.

CONTESTANT 2 Nobody.

CONTESTANT 3 Nobody.

CONTESTANT 4 Nobody.

CONTESTANT 5 Nobody.

CONTESTANT 6 Nobody.

CONTESTANT 7 Nobody.

CONTESTANT 8 Nobody.

ANNE *[insert Contestant 1's name]*, why nobody?

CONTESTANT 1 If we work together, we could probably win more money and then share it.

ANNE *[insert Contestant 2's name]*, why not vote off *[insert Contestant 7's name]*. S/he got her/his question wrong. You don't want an inept dunce like that on your team!

CONTESTANT 2 When people have difficulties, you should try to help them rather be critical of them.

ANNE Uh?! *[insert Contestant 4's name]*, only three of you got questions right. Why not neutralize these numb-skulls? There's not a brain cell between them!

CONTESTANT 4 Everyone has their strengths and weak-nesses and you have to give people a chance to show their strengths.

ANNE Strengths?! I think we'd be struggling a bit there. One of your team didn't even know what elliptical meant.

CONTESTANT 4 Did you?

ANNE Um ... *[insert Contestant 5's name]*, do you want to win *any* prize money? I wouldn't want to go anywhere near a swimming pool with you. You got a simple question wrong! So, we're hardly reeling in admiration there!

CONTESTANT 5 Well, I knew the answer but, in the heat of the moment, my mind went blank.

ANNE No change there then! *[insert Contestant 6's name]*,

you got your question correct. Why deliberately land yourself with this bunch of primitive simpletons?

CONTESTANT 6 Because they're my friends and I want them to have the money.

ANNE Oooh! Blessed are the meek for they shall inherit the earth.

CONTESTANT 6 No, it's all right, you can have it.

ANNE And, [*insert Contestant 8's name*]. You weren't exactly first in the queue when they were handing out the grey matter, were you!

BACKGROUND VOICE 1 Stitostically, stotistically, statistically we now know that nobody is about to leave with nothing.

BACKGROUND VOICE 2 Neither is nothing about to leave with nobody nor is no-one going nowhere.

BACKGROUND VOICE 1 *Non sibi, sed omnibus.*

BACKGROUND VOICE 2 Not for oneself, but for all.

7

Outlines for Further Assemblies

These can be used as teacher- or pupil-based assemblies.

Anne Frank

Give a brief outline of the story of Anne Frank:

Anne was born in 1929 and lived in Amsterdam. She was ten when the Second World War broke out. She was Jewish. In 1940, the Germans invaded Holland. There was no way for the Frank family to escape. Jews had to wear a yellow star and were subject to many other laws that only applied to Jews. Soon, the Germans started to round up Jews and sent them to concentration camps. Anne's father, Otto, narrowly escaped being caught. Following this, the Franks hid in rooms behind Otto's office, along with another Jewish family. They were cooped up there for two whole years. Before the Allied Forces liberated Amsterdam, the family was arrested and sent to concentration camps. Anne died there just before the Allied Forces reached the concentration camp.

Points you may wish to cover:

Persecution

How would you feel if you were persecuted unfairly? For example, if you had brown hair or freckles, you would be forced to wear a luminous green anorak every time you went out. Later, you would only be allowed out in this anorak between certain times and would not be allowed to own a pet. Show how the laws became stricter and stricter. What would you have done in such a situation?

Empathy

Imagine being stuck in a very small space with your family and one other family for two whole years. You can't make any noise. You can't go out. You can't be alone. You are always worried that you are going to be captured and killed. Her family had done nothing wrong but they were treated like criminals.

Hope

Despite these appalling circumstances, Anne's diary is full of hope. She looks forward to all the things she'll be able to do when she gets out. She looks out of the window at the trees and the blue sky and is happy just because they are there. 'As long as this exists – I thought – this sunshine and this cloudless sky; and as long as I can enjoy it, how can I be sad?'

Points for reflection:

Have things changed? How could this happen again? Use examples from a school context, for example, picking on someone for no reason, when people gang up on each other. Are we always generous and open towards others?

Victor Klemperer

Read excerpts from *I Shall Bear Witness: Diaries 1933–41* and *To the Bitter End: Diaries: 1942–45*. These are extremely vivid and, frankly, terrifying accounts of persecution against the Jews and would only really be suitable for an older audience.

The Jewish festival of Purim: having the courage to speak out when you know something is wrong

Start by telling or acting out the story of Esther:

Esther was born in a country called Persia, which we now know as Iran. She was Jewish and very beautiful and clever. She was an orphan. A relation called Mordecai brought her up. He was a very kind and wise man.

She was so beautiful and clever that when the King of Persia was looking for a wife, he chose Esther. This put Esther in danger, as she was Jewish and the Persians did not like the Jews. Therefore, Mordecai told her not to tell the King she was Jewish.

When Esther married the King, Mordecai went with her to the palace. He was given an important job and foiled an attempt to kill the King. This was noted in the palace records.

All went well until the King appointed a chief minister called Haman. It was Haman's job to ensure that, when the King passed, everyone bowed down. Everyone did, except Mordecai. The King was furious and, at Haman's suggestion, ordered that all Jews be rounded up and killed. Esther, who overheard this order, didn't know what to do, so sent a message to Mordecai, asking for his advice.

Mordecai suggested that she was in this position so that she could do something about it. Esther decided to try to stop the rounding up of the Jews, regardless of the consequences for her. She invites the King to an enormous banquet. The King is so pleased that he asks Esther what she would like. He tells her she can have anything, even half his kingdom. She replies that she wants him to come to another banquet and to bring Haman with him.

When the King invites Haman to the banquet, Haman thinks he must be up for promotion. This is spoilt by the sight of Mordecai sitting at the King's gate. He is so annoyed, that, coerced by his family, he decides to put Mordecai on the gallows. He builds the gallows and intends to ask the King's permission for the execution the following day.

That night, the King can't sleep. So, he has a browse through the palace records. He sees the account of Mordecai saving his life, and realizes that he hasn't rewarded him. He sends for Haman and orders that Mordecai be given one of his horses and a royal robe. Haman is not a happy man but reassures himself that at least he has the banquet to look forward to.

The second banquet takes place and, again, the

King asks Esther what she would like. She takes a deep breath, grits her teeth and says she doesn't want the Jews to be killed and that she is a Jew. The King asks who is responsible. Haman is taken to the gallows he had built for Mordecai and is executed.

The Jews are saved and Esther's bravery is remembered at the festival of Purim.

Points for reflection:

Stand up for what you know is right

Ask the pupils to imagine that everyone who supported Manchester United or believed in horoscopes was rounded up, never to be seen again. How would they feel? Would they try to stop this? Would they dare say anything in case they too were rounded up? Say that this was the dilemma facing Esther.

Change things when you have the opportunity

Remind them that Mordecai tells Esther that perhaps she has been made queen in order to help the Jewish people. Point out that there are times when we too are given the chance to do something important to change things. Give examples: choosing a right action when a wrong one would have been easier or safer; helping someone when no-one else dared; sticking up for someone whom no-one else liked.

The Hindu festival of Holi

This is another case of good triumphing over evil. Tell or get pupils to act out the following story:

Once upon a time, there was a King. He was cruel and wicked. He thought he was so amazing that he wanted to be worshipped as a god by his people. This they did. This King had a son called Prahlada who knew his father wasn't a god and refused to worship him. Instead, he worshipped a real god called Vishnu. This made the King very cross. He ordered a herd of elephants to trample Prahlada. Prahlada was un-harmed, because Vishnu protected him.

The King had an equally unsavoury sister called Holika. Holika had magic powers, which meant she could not be harmed by fire. The King and Holika took Prahlada to the top of an enormous bonfire and Holika and Prahlada jumped in. Contrary to expectations, it was Holika that was burned rather than Prahlada, because the god Vishnu has protected him and destroyed Holika's powers. Prahlada was safe because he put his faith in a real god and, therefore, good has triumphed over evil.

Point out that Holi is a spring festival in India and that bonfires are a key element of the festivities, not only because of the story but because bonfires represent light after the darkness of winter. Bonfires remind Hindus that winter is ending. Hindus believe that bonfires offer protection from harm and babies are often carried around them during the Holi celebrations. Grains are roasted on the fires and this is a way of celebrating and giving thanks to the god. Holi is a time of hope and new beginnings.

Sometimes the celebrations are completely riotous and involve squirting others with water, coloured paints or dyes. This is supposed to symbolize fertility and springtime. There is another connection with the god Krishna who was rather partial to practical jokes and, allegedly, a milkmaid threw dye over him. You could draw a connection with April Fools' Day.

Haile Selassie

Get your hands on some Bob Marley music! This would be an assembly about equality. Give a summary of his life:

Haile Selassie was born on 23rd July 1892. In 1930, he became emperor of Ethiopia and was given the title Ras Tafari. Rastafarianism was born. Rastafarians believe that God shows himself on earth from time to time and that Haile Selassie was God in human form. They believed that he was a descendant of King Solomon. A key belief is that Ras Tafari will help black people who can trace their routes back to the slave trade return to Africa.

Explain that Rastafarianism originated in the Caribbean where many people are descended from Africans. A long time ago, they were taken away from their homes in Africa to work as slaves in the Caribbean. The Rastafarian faith believes that Haile Selassie was important because he spoke up for black people who had suffered from slavery. Therefore, it is very important for them to speak out against situations that are unfair. Perhaps this is why they are also vegetarians.

Finally, get the pupils to think about times when people are treated unfairly because of the colour of their skin, or because of what they believe. Why? How might it feel? Stress the importance of peace and understanding between people, whatever their differences. Mention people who are currently working to bring peace and understanding in the world. Kofi Annan springs to mind.

Le Petit Prince by Antoine de Saint-Exupéry

I love this masterpiece! What a treasure trove! Buy a copy now! Snippets of this little gem can be read or acted out. It's secret is in its simplicity. You can draw all sorts of themes from this book: judging by appearances, the ephemeral nature of outer beauty, the importance of facing reality (however hard this may be!). It will take you ten minutes to read and the ideas will bounce off the page!

Sticks and stones will break my bones but words could hurt me more

Show the pupils your favourite kitchen knife (preferably the biggest and sharpest!). Point out the various uses of a knife. Ideally, do something impressive to show them just how sharp it is. Keep well away from that rather annoying child in Year 6 or the brown-nosing colleague! The temptation may well be too much. Then, go on to point out that although the knife is very useful, it is also very dangerous. Say it was given to you as a present. Tell them that they have all been given presents that can be very useful and dangerous: their minds and tongues. These presents, like the knife, need to be used with care. They can be used as weapons to hurt or we can used them like a first-aid kit – to heal.

You could end with the following two quotations from the Bible: 'Thoughtless words can act as deeply as a sword but wise words can heal' (Proverbs 12:18), and 'Use helpful words, not harmful ones: words which will build people up and do good to those who hear them' (Ephesians 4:29).

Jealousy

Explain to the pupils that dangerous things often have warning signs on them to show that they are dangerous, for example, bottles of bleach, beaches where there are dangerous currents and railway lines. Animals also show that they may be dangerous, by growling or baring their teeth. Then, tell them that there are some dangerous things that do not have a danger or warning sign on them. One such thing is jealousy. Give examples of why one person might be jealous of another – for their looks, intelligence, possessions or friends. Tell them that one of the reasons Jesus was crucified was because the Roman authorities were jealous of the influence that Jesus had over the people. Then, you might read or act out the story of Joseph and his brothers.

Points for reflection:
1. We should treat jealousy like a dangerous substance that has no warning signs, and 2. Sometimes we can't help feeling jealous but we can help how we behave.

You could end with biblical quotations: Proverbs 27:4, Corinthians 13:4, James 3:14, 16.

All good things come to he who waits

Lent is a good time for this one as it features the account of Jesus' 40-day session in the wilderness.

Set the scene: Palestine, during Jesus' lifetime. John the Baptist, between mouthfuls of locusts and honey, is urging the people to get ready for the Messiah. Read the account of Jesus' baptism (Mark 1:9–12). This marked a turning point in Jesus' life. He was no longer a mere carpenter. He realized that he had higher things to do. He goes to the wilderness to think things through. Script the account of Jesus being taunted by the Devil and get three pupils to act it out (narrator, Jesus, Devil). Use Matthew 4:1–11, as it is the most detailed account.

Points for reflection:

Life-changing experiences

Jesus' baptism was obviously a life-changing experience. It is when he realizes that he has knowledge of a deeper truth and some kind of inner power. Have the pupils or their friends and families had life-changing experiences? Did they use them for the good of others? Give examples of any life-changing experiences you have had.

Taking words out of context

Demonstrate that the Devil tries to tempt Jesus by quoting the Scriptures and twisting their meanings. Have the pupils ever been subjected to this kind of temptation, perhaps by friends encouraging them to do something they know they shouldn't? Can they see how dangerous words can be when they are misused?

Resisting temptation

Get them to imagine what it would have been like to be in the wilderness for 40 days and nights, without any home comforts at all. Could they suffer the heat, cold, hunger and thirst for such a long period, as well as being hassled by the voice of temptation? Would they cope? How? Say that everyday life is strewn with temptations and that we all must be ready to resist them.

The importance of waiting for things

It would have been much easier for Jesus to go straight out and preach, rather than stride manfully off into the wilderness. He had the wisdom to know that he needed thinking time first. There are times when we need to take time and think things over rather than rush in like the proverbial bull. There is a skill of knowing the right time to do or say things. What examples can they think of in their own lives? Give examples of your own, if you can bear it!

Using power responsibly

Jesus knows that he is given power at his baptism. It would have been possible for him to carry out all the Devil's offers and suggestions. Instead, he used his power to resist the Devil. We all have power over friends, family and other acquaintances. Other people have power over us. This power can be used to get material things, influence situations or even to avoid trouble. We must all learn to use it in the right way – one that respects the needs of others.

Useful Websites

This is by no means an extensive list and the websites mentioned are not necessarily the best ones. I have found them all very helpful on the way, both for writing assemblies and researching this book.

Public speaking

www.fearofpublicspeaking.net
www.instantspeakingsuccess.com

General assemblies websites

www.assemblies.org
www.perfectiononwheels.com : educational assembly ideas on safety and drugs.
www.schoolassemblies.btinternet.co.uk

Scripture from other religions

www.krislon.net : the story of Rama and others
www.sdmart.org/exhibition-binney-rama1.html : some lovely illustrations of the Rama story from San Diego Museum of Art.
www.watthai.net : Indian folklore and religious stories.

Calendar of religious festivals

www.startinbusiness.co.uk/hols/festivals.htm : a comprehensive calendar that gives you the exact dates for each year. Also gives calendars up to 2010 and Easter dates up to 2005. National anthems. Saints' days.
www.support4learning.org.uk/shap/calend4a.htm

Information on major world religions

www.omsakthi.org/religions.html : a really clear, succinct overview with some excellent links.

Ancient mythology

www.hippy.freeserve.co.uk : has some excellent lists. Caution! Very easy to be sidetracked on this eccentric little site!
http://web.uvic.ca/grs/bowman/myth

Interpretations of fairy stories

www.novelguide.com : explores the metaphors in fairy tales and children's stories.

National days

www.breastcancercampaign.org : National Breast Cancer Awareness Day
www.curryworld.co.uk : National Curry Day
www.doit.org.uk : Make a Difference Day
www.poetrysociety.org.uk/npd : National Poetry Day
www.un.org/ecosocdev/women : International Women's Day

Saints

www.catholic.org/saints : check out their fun facts page for some really quirky snippets.
www.hillsdale.edu/dept/Phil&Rel/Biography
www.ottawainnercityministries.ca/biographies
www.pitt.edu/~eflst4.htm
www.re-xs.ac.uk/cupboard

Offbeat and child-friendly news stores

www.anorak.co.uk
www.bbc.co.uk : follow links to 'Planet Tabloid'.
www.bbc.co.uk/cbbcnews : this is the Newsround website. Have a look at the 'Your Comments' and message boards to see what's making the little cherubs tick.

Remarkable individuals

Anne Frank : *www.annefrank.nl*
Evelyn Glennie : *www.evelyn.co.uk/hearing.htm*
Ellen MacArthur : *www.ellenmacarthur.com*
Iris Murdoch : *www.irismurdoch.plus.com*
Paula Radcliffe : *www.sport.guardian.co.uk*
J.K. Rowling : *www.csi-net.net/~svderark/lexicon/faq/faq_rowling.html*
Haile Selassie : *www.bobartinstitute.edu/Sellassie*

Spiritual material

www.allspirit.co.uk: poetry, readings, reflections, quotations. An excellent site for the prayer shy.

Miscellaneous religious websites

www.cafod.org.uk
www.misslink.org/children
www.prayingeachday.org
www.vatican.va

Charities

www.fundraisingdirectory.com
www.globalgang.org.uk : Christian Aid's children's website.

Making props

www.dltk-kids.com/crafts
www.kids.com/crafts

Bibliography

The following tomes reside on my own sagging book-shelves. I hope that you find some of them useful.

Public speaking

The Oxford Union Guide to Successful Public Speaking: The Definitive Guide from the Definitive Authority, Hughes, P. and Phillips, B.
Stand Up and Talk to 1,000 People and Enjoy It, Witz, M.

Ethics

The Plain Man's Guide to Ethics, Barclay, W.

Literature

Everyone has their favourites, particularly when it comes to children's literature. These are the ones I have found most inspiring and include those that my children particularly love. Obviously, you'll have your favourites too. If you enjoy a book, use it!

Jonathan Livingston Seagull, Bach, R.
The Basketball Diaries, Carroll, J.
The Prophet, Gibran, K.

The Tao of Pooh, Hoff, B.
The Te of Piglet, Hoff, B.
I Am David, Holm, A.
Just So Stories, Kipling, R.
The Chronicles of Narnia, Lewis, C.S.
Winnie the Pooh: The Complete Collection of Stories and Poems, Milne, A.A.
The Little Prince, Saint-Exupéry, A. de
Pooh and the Philosophers, Tyerman Williams, J.
Wilson, J.:
   The Story of Tracy Beaker (life in a children's home)
   The Suitcase Kid (divorce, custody)
   Buried Alive! (bullying)
   Sleepovers (disability)
   Vicky Angel (bereavement)
   Dustbin Baby (fostering, adoption)
   Secrets (class barriers, broken homes)
   Lola Rose (domestic violence)

Rowling, J.K.:
   Harry Potter and the Philosopher's Stone
   Harry Potter and the Chamber of Secrets
   Harry Potter and the Prisoner of Azkaban
   Harry Potter and the Goblet of Fire
   Harry Potter and the Order of the Phoenix

Interpretation of dreams and stories

Understanding Dreams: What They Are and How to Read Them, Dee, N.
Interpretation of Fairy Tales, Wilkinson, R.
The Forgotten Language: An Introduction to the Understanding of Dreams, Fairy Tales, and Myths, Fromm, E.
Dream Detective, Robinson, C. and Boot, A.
The Dreamer's Dictionary, Robinson, S. and Corbett, T.

The Interpretation of Fairy Tales, Franz, M-L. von

Anne Frank

Anne Frank's Story: Her Life Retold for Children, Lee, C.A.
Anne Frank: Beyond the Diary, Rol, R. von der

Proverbs and Prayers

Dreams Alive: Prayers by Teenagers, Koch, C. (ed.)
The Languid Goat is Always Thin: The World's Strangest Proverbs, Arnott, S.
Inspirations: A Personal Collection of Poems, Proverbs and Quotations, Dobson, D. (ed.)
The Concise Oxford Dictionary of Proverbs, Simpson, J. (ed.)

The Ten Commandments of Assemblies

And the DfES spake all these words, saying, 'I am thy Minister for Education, which have brought thee out of the land of Teacher Autonomy, into the house of Government Prescription.'

Thou shalt:

1. Deliver 'Collective Worship' that will be daily.

2. Make it wholly or mainly Christian in character.

3. Do so in such a manner that it is acceptable to the whole community, staff and pupils.

4. Include a variety of elements at different times.

5. Involve the pupils.

6. Be a rushing stream of inspiration, full of spiritually enriching ideas.

7. [Delete as applicable]:

   (a) Be fervently religious and zealously keen to share this with your fellow human beings.
   (b) Pretend to be fervently religious and zealously keen not to share this with your fellow human beings.

8. Not suffer from stage fright.

9. Not take a sickie/emigrate/commit suicide on the day in question.

10. Have to take calming measures/it in your stride.

Assemblies Made Easy

And all the teachers saw the thunderings, and the lightnings, and the noise of the trumpet and the mountain smoking: and when the people saw it, they removed and stood afar off. And headed for the staff room kettle.